simple bible.

Understanding the heart of God and our relationship with Him simply by looking at His Word.

Daryl Merrill

Copyright © 2020 Daryl Merrill

All rights reserved.

ISBN: 9781090784766

simple bible.

Understanding the heart of God and our relationship
with Him simply by looking at His Word.

Daryl Merrill

DEDICATED TO
MY CHRISTIAN LIFE FAMILY

I'm grateful we get to study and live God's Word together.

CONTENTS

About This Book	1
Old Testament	5
New Testament	85
A Final Thought	141
Salvation Prayer	143
About The Author	145

ABOUT THIS BOOK

I love the Bible. I love that God revealed what He wanted us to know in His Word. We don't have to wonder what God is like. We don't have to guess about what He desires for our life. He makes it plain and simple.

By looking at one verse from every book of the Bible we will discover who God is, what He says about us, and how it all impacts our lives. This is more than just another Bible study, this is a look at the very heart of the God who is crazy about you. Ready to learn more? Let's dive in.

What comes into our minds when we think about God is the most important thing about us.

—AW Tozer

OLD TESTAMENT

The story of the Bible isn't primarily about the desire of people to be with God; it's the desire of God to be with people.

—John Ortberg

Genesis.

Good.

"...you meant evil against me, but God meant it for good..."
Genesis 50:20a ESV

It's simple.

- The Bible is God's story.
- God reveals Himself through His Word.
- Genesis tells the story of our beginning.
- About our Creator who loves His creation and calls it good.
- About a God of relationship.
- About a God of covenants.
- About a God who is faithful from the first to the last, even when we are not.
- About a God who is good.
- About a God who promises good to you and me.
- No matter if we lose our way.
- No matter the mistakes we make.
- No matter how broken we are.
- No matter what others do to us.
- No matter how desperate the situation.
- God was WITH Joseph in the pit and prison, before He led him to the palace.
- We are tempted to think God isn't good, or question His motives, but His Word assures us that He IS good and His love endures forever.
- God's plan for us is to bless us. (see Genesis 12:2-3)
- "God meant it for good," means God is ALWAYS at work for our good. Always.

Though our feelings come and go, God's love for us does not.

— CS Lewis

Exodus.

Who God is.

The Lord passed before him and proclaimed, "The Lord, the Lord, a God merciful and gracious, slow to anger, and abounding in steadfast love and faithfulness, keeping steadfast love for thousands, forgiving iniquity and transgression and sin..."

Exodus 34:6-7a ESV

It's simple.

- God reveals Himself through His Word.
- Moses asked to see God.
- Not since Adam in the Garden had God walked with man.
- When God shows up how does God describe Himself?
- Merciful.
- Gracious.
- Slow to anger.
- Abounding in steadfast love.
- Faithful.
- Forgiving.
- This is God in His own words.
- He is the great I AM. (see Exodus 3:14)
- God is everything and all that we need.
- God delivers us from sin and bondage and reveals Himself to us.
- Sin separates and destroys our lives and relationship.
- God forgives, sets free, and restores.
- Follow the One who is merciful, gracious, patient, loving, faithful, and forgiving.

God loves you as you are, and not as you should be.

— Brennan Manning

Leviticus.

Fire.

"Remember, the fire must be kept burning on the altar at all times. It must never go out."

Leviticus 6:13 NIV

It's simple.

- The fire in this verse represents our relationship with God.
- It's an ongoing relationship that must never burn out.
- Great care is taken to tend the fire.
- Good relationships take great care.
- Leviticus is a book of rules and obedience.
- We are called to be holy as He is holy. (see Leviticus 19:2)
- Being holy is about belonging to God.
- God calls you His own.
- You belong to God.
- You are His child.
- Relationships are not a list of rules to follow, they're about belonging to one another.
- Relationships are about listening, sharing, and commitment.
- Take care of your relationship with God.
- God is committed to keeping the fire burning.
- Draw near to the God who is passionate about a relationship with you.

Do not look for evil. Look for the goodness of God all around you. As you look for signs of His Presence, many more opportunities will occur for you to bless people and share God's true nature.

— Graham Cooke

Numbers.

You Can Count on God.

The Lord answered Moses, "Is the Lord's arm too short? Now you will see whether or not what I say will come true for you..."

Numbers 11:23 NIV

It's simple.

- God wants you to count on Him.
- God is with you.
- God is faithful.
- God is able.
- What God says He will do, He will do.
- God will fight your battles.
- God will give you the victory.
- He did it for the children of Israel and He'll do it for you.
- *"Rise up, O Lord, and let Your enemies be scattered."* Numbers 10:35 MEV
- Stop looking at how big your enemies are and see how BIG your God is.
- You can count on God. Always and forever.

This is true faith, a living confidence in the goodness of God.

— Martin Luther

Deuteronomy.

Blessed.

"And all these blessings shall come upon you and overtake you, if you obey the voice of the Lord your God."
Deuteronomy 28:2 ESV

It's simple.

- God is a God of blessing.
- Actually, God is a God of abundant blessing.
- God's Word reminds us again and again of the blessings that come from following and obeying God.
- God doesn't curse, He blesses.
- Blessing follows obedience.
- Disobedience brings consequences.
- God always has your best interest in mind.
- When you obey, God's blessings are going to chase you down.
- When you disobey you will experience the curse of sin.
- It's YOUR choice.
- Believe and follow God's Word and there is a blessing.
- Choosing to ignore or disobey brings curses.
- It's your choice.
- God wants to bless you in a cursed world.
- Just obey.
- God doesn't want you cursed, He wants to see you blessed to a thousand generations.
- Don't blame God, follow Him, and BE BLESSED.

Grace is not reserved for good people; grace underscores the goodness of God.

— Andy Stanley

Joshua.

Be Strong and Courageous.

"Have I not commanded you? Be strong and courageous. Do not be frightened, and do not be dismayed, for the Lord your God is with you wherever you go."
Joshua 1:9 ESV

It's simple.

- We are commanded to be strong.
- We are commanded to be courageous.
- We are commanded to not be afraid.
- We are commanded to not be anxious.
- We are commanded to not be disillusioned.
- Why?
- Because God is WITH us.
- The top command in the Bible is "Do not be afraid."
- Craig Groeschel said, "What you fear reveals where you trust God the least."
- Our powerful and present God makes us strong and courageous.
- With God on our side, we don't have to be afraid and anxious.

We do not have to be bashful with God.

— Teresa of Avila

Judges.

Mighty Warrior.

When the angel of the Lord appeared to Gideon, he said, "The Lord is with you, mighty warrior."

Judges 6:12 NIV

It's simple.

- God sees our true identity from the very beginning.
- Gideon felt weak, small, and conquered.
- God saw him as mighty.
- God sees who we are in Him.
- He saw a young, wild Simon as Peter the Rock. (see John 1:42)
- When we see who we are in God everything changes.
- Our true identity lies in Him.
- Don't forget where our power comes from.
- Follow His battle plan.
- Do not worry about what other people think of you.
- Don't worry how it looks in the natural.
- God's got good plans for you.
- He is making you into His mighty warrior.

The primary purpose of reading the Bible is not to know the Bible but to know God.

— James Merritt

Ruth.

Sustainer.

"He will renew your life and sustain you in your old age."
Ruth 4:15a NIV

It's simple.

- God is faithful.
- His promises last a lifetime.
- God is always watching out for us from the beginning to the end.
- Even in the midst of tragedy God has good plan.
- What seems like the end may just be the beginning.
- God will bring the right people into your life at the right time.
- When you commit yourself to God and His people, He commits Himself to you. (see Ruth 1:16)
- God WILL take good care of you, your WHOLE life.

Our God is a compassionate God.

— Leslie Merrill

1 Samuel.

Heart.

"The Lord does not look at the things people look at. People look at the outward appearance, but the Lord looks at the heart."

1 Samuel 16:7b NIV

It's simple.

- It's all about the heart.
- It's not just about what we do and don't do.
- As human beings, we tend to judge by outer appearance because that's all we can see.
- God goes much deeper.
- God looks beyond the action or inaction and looks at the attitude of the heart.
- Our heart impacts EVERYTHING in our life.
- *"Guard your heart above all else, for it is the source of life."* Proverbs 4:23 CSB
- Check your heart today.
- Ask God for His help.
- God loves you!
- God is love.
- Love God with all your heart.
- He desires you to have a heart after Him.

Each and everyday we must allow God to continually soften our hearts so that it beats for what His heart beats for—people.

— Christine Caine

2 Samuel.

Shield and Refuge.

As for God, his way is perfect: The Lord's word is flawless; he shields all who take refuge in him.

2 Samuel 22:31 NIV

It's simple.

- You can trust God.
- His way is perfect.
- He knows the beginning to the end.
- There is no detail God has not thought of.
- You can take God at His word.
- His Word is flawless.
- He is our shield.
- He is our refuge.
- When we go God's way we are never alone.
- Don't do life on your own.
- Don't go your own way.
- We're not meant to be isolated.
- Your strength and knowledge are limited. God's are not.
- God always takes care of those He loves.
- Remember God loves you. His way is perfect. Follow Him.

God didn't get stuck with you; He chose you.

— Levi Lusko

1 Kings.

Gentle Whisper.

The Lord said, "Go out and stand on the mountain in the presence of the Lord, for the Lord is about to pass by." Then a great and powerful wind tore the mountains apart and shattered the rocks before the Lord, but the Lord was not in the wind. After the wind there was an earthquake, but the Lord was not in the earthquake. After the earthquake came a fire, but the Lord was not in the fire. And after the fire came a gentle whisper. When Elijah heard it, he pulled his cloak over his face and went out and stood at the mouth of the cave.

1 Kings 19:11-13a NIV

It's simple.

- God wants to speak to us.
- God wants us to know His presence.
- God is mighty and powerful.
- God can show up any way He wants to and will show up any way He wants to.
- In a great and powerful wind. In an earthquake. In a fire.
- But more often than not God shows up in a still small voice.
- A gentle whisper.
- God is always at a state of peace.
- If God speaks in a still small voice we must quiet our hearts and minds to hear His voice and know His presence.
- When God does show up (and He will) make sure you come out to meet Him like Elijah did.

Grace is God's unilateral decision to love.

— AJ Sherrill

2 Kings.

God Hears Your Prayers.

Go back and tell Hezekiah, the ruler of my people, "This is what the Lord, the God of your father David, says: I have heard your prayer and seen your tears; I will heal you."

2 Kings 20:5 NIV

It's simple.

- There is power in prayer.
- Hezekiah knew the power of prayer.
- Whenever he was in trouble he prayed.
- When his enemies were attacking he prayed.
- *And Hezekiah prayed to the Lord: "Lord, the God of Israel, enthroned between the cherubim, you alone are God over all the kingdoms of the earth. You have made heaven and earth. Give ear, Lord, and hear; open your eyes, Lord, and see...Now, Lord our God, deliver us from his hand, so that all the kingdoms of the earth may know that you alone, Lord, are God."* 2 Kings 19:15-16, 19 NIV
- God heard, answered, and rescued Hezekiah time and time again.
- God hears your prayers.
- God sees your tears.
- He knows exactly what you need and He's waiting for you to call on Him.
- Your prayers matter.
- The only time Hezekiah struggled was late in life when he forgot about God.
- Don't forget about God.
- Pray today!

If it's not too good to be true, it's not God.

— Graham Cooke

1 Chronicles.

God Isn't Hiding.

"And you, my son Solomon, acknowledge the God of your father, and serve him with wholehearted devotion and with a willing mind, for the Lord searches every heart and understands every desire and every thought. If you seek him, he will be found by you; but if you forsake him, he will reject you forever."

1 Chronicles 28:9 NIV

It's simple.

- Finding God is up to you.
- But remember, God isn't hiding.
- If you want to find Him you will.
- If you don't, you won't.
- How do you find God?
- It's all about the heart.
- Serve Him.
- Be devoted.
- Be willing.
- Be wholehearted.
- Don't reject Him.
- He's searching your heart and mind.
- He's waiting to be found by those who seek Him with all their heart.

I am not who I think I am, I am who God says I am.

— Jarrid Wilson

2 Chronicles.

The Battle Belongs to the Lord.

This is what the Lord says: "Do not be afraid! Don't be discouraged by this mighty army, for the battle is not yours, but God's."

2 Chronicles 20:15b. NIV

It's simple.

- God tells us again and again AND AGAIN throughout His Word to not be afraid.
- God also says, "Don't be discouraged."
- Shouldn't we be afraid?
- Aren't there a lot of very real things in this life that should discourage us?
- Aren't there many battles that we face?
- Yes. Yes. And yes.
- BUT God wants you to know that the battle is NOT yours, it's His.
- And the Lord NEVER loses.
- God is with you.
- He will never leave you.
- God is fighting for you.
- There WILL be victory because the battle belongs to the Lord.
- So be bold, full of faith, and pray.
- This is how we fight our battles.

Enrich your soul in the great goodness of God: The Father is your table, the Son is your food, and the Holy Spirit waits on you and then makes His dwelling in you.

— St. Catherine of Siena

Ezra.

Study and Obey.

Now Ezra had determined in his heart to study the law of the Lord, obey it, and teach its statutes and ordinances in Israel.
                                                                Ezra 7:10 HCSB

It's simple.

- Ezra is one of the most important characters in the Bible.
- Scholars credit him with assembling the Old Testament Canon.
- He helped reestablish the Jewish people after the Babylonian exile.
- His life was spent studying the Law of the Lord with all of his heart.
- He didn't just study, he obeyed.
- He taught it to others.
- Love God's Word.
- Study God's Word.
- Obey God's Word.
- Share God's Word.
- *"The law of the LORD is perfect, refreshing the soul. The statutes of the LORD are trustworthy, making wise the simple."* Psalms 19:7 NIV

No matter what storm you face, you need to know that God loves you. He has not abandoned you.

— Franklin Graham

Nehemiah.

Study and Obey.

"...the joy of the Lord is your strength."
Nehemiah 8:10b NIV

It's simple.

- Nehemiah was a man of prayer and obedience.
- He followed God and brought others along with him.
- Together they built, fought, and persevered.
- When the people heard the law of God read out loud they worshipped and wept.
- They took the Word of God seriously.
- But God desired His people to rejoice in His presence.
- It was time for joy.
- God's Word is meant to heal. (see Psalms 107:20)
- Jesus said, *"Blessed are those who mourn, for they will be comforted."* Matthew 5:4 NIV
- *"Weeping may last through the night, but joy comes in the morning."* Psalms 30:5 NIV
- God is a God of forgiveness and restoration.
- God has done great things for His people in the past and now in the present.
- When God is with us and for us, that's a reason to rejoice.
- God is strong!
- He is our strength!
- He is our joy!

God is not figured out. He is revealed.

— Steve Sampson

Esther.

Calling.

"For if you keep silent at this time, relief and deliverance will rise for the Jews from another place, but you and your father's house will perish. And who knows whether you have not come to the kingdom for such a time as this?"

Esther 4:14 NIV

It's simple.

- You are a part of God's Kingdom plan.
- God gives each of us a calling.
- He wants to use us where we are.
- God's will WILL be done.
- The question is…will we choose to be a part of His plan?
- Pray about and partake in God's plan.
- He wants to use you for such a time as this!

There are things you can do that will cause people to write you off. But there is nothing you can do (or fail to do) that will ever cause God to write you off.

— Tullian Tchividjian

Job.

He is God. You are not.

"Where were you when I laid the earth's foundation? Tell me, if you understand."

Job 38:4 NIV

It's simple.

- You don't know everything. But God does.
- You can't do everything. But God can.
- You can't see behind the scenes. But God is there, working.
- You may or may not know what to do. But God always does.
- Your plan may or may not work. But God's will.
- You may or may not win. But God will.
- You don't know how to make things right. But God does.
- You can't save yourself. But God can.
- You worry. But God doesn't.
- Trust Him. God's got this.
- He's God. You are not.

God is bigger than whatever is stressing you out!

— Kimberly Jones-Pothier

Psalms.

The Lord is my Shepherd.

The Lord is my best friend and my shepherd. I always have more than enough.

Psalms 23:1 TPT

It's simple.

- God is my Shepherd and Friend.
- God is my source.
- God is my supply.
- I will lack no good thing.
- He takes care of me.
- He makes (lets) me rest.
- He leads me in peace, ease, and refreshing.
- He restores my soul and renews my strength.
- He guides me in His way because I belong to Him.
- He is close to me, even in my darkest moments.
- He watches out for me, no matter what it takes.
- He feeds me.
- He protects me.
- He gives me favor and honor.
- He heals me.
- He blesses me.
- He pursues me all my life until I'm with Him forever!

God doesn't consult your past, so why do you consult your past about your future?

— Jay Haizlip

Proverbs.

Wisdom.

The fear of the Lord is the beginning of knowledge, but fools despise wisdom and instruction.
Proverbs 1:7 NIV

It's simple.

- God knows what's best. He is Wisdom.
- God, our creator, gives us wisdom for life.
- You can do life your way or His way.
- His way is always best.
- Ask God for His wisdom.
- He will always answer that prayer. (see James 1:5)
- Wisdom is God's gift to you.
- You can't and won't ever go wrong obeying God.

God loves each of us as if there were only one of us.

— St. Augustine

Ecclesiastes.

Life and Eternity.

He has made everything beautiful in its time. He has also set eternity in the human heart; yet no one can fathom what God has done from beginning to end.
Ecclesiastes 3:11 NIV

It's simple.

- There is a time for everything.
- *"There is a time for everything, and a season for every activity under the heavens."* Ecclesiastes 3:1 NIV
- God knows the times and seasons of life.
- He knows everything from the beginning to the end.
- He will guide us through them perfectly.
- Our only job is to fear and follow Him.
- *"Fear God and keep His commandments, for this is the whole duty of man."* Ecclesiastes 12:13a MEV
- Then we get to enjoy eternity with Him!

I have given God countless reasons not to love me. None of them has been strong enough to change Him.

— Paul Washer

Song of Solomon.

Beloved.

"I am my beloved's and my beloved is mine."
The Song of Solomon 6:3a ESV

It's simple.

- God loves YOU.
- YOU are God's beloved.
- This is who YOU are.
- This is YOUR identity.
- God desires YOUR love.
- God wants a relationship with YOU.
- There is nothing more special or valuable to Him.

Obedience deepens our intimacy with Jesus. If we want to know the Father, we must not only love Him, but also obey Him.

— John Wimber

Isaiah.

God is love.

So the Lord must wait for you to come to him so he can show you his love and compassion. For the Lord is a faithful God. Blessed are those who wait for his help.
Isaiah 30:18 NLT

It's simple.

- Jesus quoted Isaiah so much so that it is often referred to as the fifth Gospel.
- Isaiah shows us the heart of God.
- God wants to show you love and compassion.
- This is God's heart for you!
- This is God's first response.
- God is waiting for you to come to Him so He can bless you with His help.

God bestows His blessings without discrimination. The followers of Jesus are children of God, and they should manifest the family likeness by doing good to all, even to those who deserve the opposite.

— FF Bruce

Jeremiah.

God's plans for you are good.

"For I know the plans I have for you," declares the Lord, "plans to prosper you and not to harm you, plans to give you hope and a future. Then you will call on me and come and pray to me, and I will listen to you. You will seek me and find me when you seek me with all your heart."
Jeremiah 29:11-13 NIV

It's simple.

- These are the words of God through the prophet Jeremiah.
- Jeremiah was known as the "weeping prophet" because he was mourning the coming judgment of God upon His people.
- Even in the midst of all the doom and gloom Jeremiah prophesies hope.
- Even though captivity for God's people was coming, it wasn't the end of their story.
- God doesn't harm His people.
- God wants to prosper His people.
- God is a giving God.
- God is a good God.
- God lets His people know there is ALWAYS a hope and future.
- Even in the most difficult parts of life, even when we don't understand.
- God will ALWAYS listen when we call on Him.
- You can ALWAYS find God when you truly look for Him.
- When you come to God, His arms are wide open.
- Just pray today.

However many blessings we expect from God, His infinite liberality will always exceed all our wishes and our thoughts.

— John Calvin

Lamentations.

Every day you wake up blessed.

The faithful love of the Lord never ends! His mercies never cease. Great is his faithfulness; his mercies begin afresh each morning. I say to myself, "The Lord is my inheritance; therefore, I will hope in him!" The Lord is good to those who depend on him, to those who search for him. So it is good to wait quietly for salvation from the Lord.
Lamentations 3:22-26 NLT

It's simple.

- In the midst of Jeremiah's lament there is HOPE.
- There is always hope.
- This is the heart of God.
- God, in His Word, always encourages us toward faith.
- God is faithful.
- God's love is great.
- God's compassion never fails.
- God's grace is new EVERY day.
- Even in the worst times…every day you wake up blessed.
- God is our supply.
- Wait quietly for God's salvation.
- No one is cast off forever.
- Put your hope in Him.
- God doesn't bring affliction and grief, God brings compassion and joy.
- Life is hard, but God is good. Always.
- As the song says, "Great is Thy faithfulness."

God is completely sovereign. God is infinite in wisdom. God is perfect in love. God in His love always wills what is best for us. In His wisdom He always knows what is best, and in His sovereignty He has the power to bring it about.

— Jerry Bridges

Ezekiel.

A New Heart.

"And I will give you a new heart, and I will put a new spirit in you. I will take out your stony, stubborn heart and give you a tender, responsive heart."

Ezekiel 36:26 NLT

It's simple.

- God loves you just the way you are, but He loves you too much to leave you that way.
- God wants to make you new.
- No matter how broken the "old" you is, God's ultimate plan is to make all things new. (see Revelation 21:5)
- God is all about the heart. (see 1 Samuel 16:7)
- He wants to give you a new heart.
- A soft heart toward Him.
- A new heart changes everything.
- We can't change our heart, but He can.
- It's a gift from Him to anyone who asks.
- He can soften the stony, stubborn heart.
- Pray that God gives you a tender, responsive heart.
- That is a prayer God will ALWAYS answer.
- God wants to be with you, and you with Him.
- Here's more from Ezekiel… *"My dwelling place will be with them; I will be their God, and they will be my people." Ezekiel 37:27 NIV*

The goodness of God is infinitely more wonderful than we will ever be able to comprehend.

— AW Tozer

Daniel.

God is with you in the fire.

He said, "Look! I see four men walking around in the fire, unbound and unharmed, and the fourth looks like a son of the gods."

Daniel 3:25 NIV

It's simple.

- Daniel's friends, Shadrach, Meshach, and Abednego, decided to follow God in a foreign land no matter the cost.
- When their allegiance was tested they stood firm. They would not bow to an idol.
- Would God save them? Maybe. Maybe not. But it didn't matter.
- They would worship God alone.
- When they were thrown into a literal fire Jesus was with them.
- They weren't alone. God was with them.
- And God is with you!
- When God is with you, you can withstand the fire, no matter how hot it may be.

When we are broken because of increased hardship, we simply have to trust in the goodness of God.

— Steve Farrar

Hosea.

God receives real repentance.

"Come, let us return to the Lord. He has torn us to pieces but he will heal us; he has injured us but he will bind up our wounds. After two days he will revive us; on the third day he will restore us, that we may live in his presence. Let us acknowledge the Lord; let us press on to acknowledge him. As surely as the sun rises, he will appear; he will come to us like the winter rains, like the spring rains that water the earth."
"For I desire mercy, not sacrifice, and acknowledgment of God rather than burnt offerings."

Hosea 6:1-3, 6 NIV

It's simple.
- God's people, Israel, knew they needed to repent.
- They had turned their backs on God and been unfaithful.
- No matter how far they strayed, they knew God would forgive, revive, and restore them.
- Their plan was to make a quick sacrifice to God and in two or three days God would make everything better.
- The problem with their plan was God wasn't looking for the sacrifice.
- He was looking for relationship.
- This isn't about making a sacrifice to a dead pagan idol to make everything better, it was about returning to a relationship with the living God who loved them even in their unfaithfulness.
- Repentance literally means "to turn around."
- God isn't looking for insincere sacrifices to get you out of a jam, He's looking for you to repent, and return to Him.
- God's love is too great for cheap repentance.
- He wants everyone in an authentic heartfelt relationship with Him.

For God is good - or rather, of all goodness He is the Fountainhead.

— Athanasius of Alexandria

Joel.

God wants to forgive you.

"Don't tear your clothing in your grief, but tear your hearts instead. Return to the Lord your God, for he is merciful and compassionate, slow to get angry and filled with unfailing love. He is eager to relent and not punish."

Joel 2:13 NLT

It's simple.

- God is a God of blessing, not a God of punishment.
- God is merciful.
- God is compassionate.
- God is slow to anger.
- God is full of unfailing love.
- God wants to forgive you.
- God is looking for you to return to Him.
- He's not looking for a "sorry," He's looking for your heart.
- And when you give Him your heart, He will bring his blessings upon you.

...the goodness of God is the highest object of prayer and it reaches down to our lowest need.

— Julian of Norwich

Amos.

God speaks to YOU.

"He who forms the mountains, who creates the wind, and who reveals his thoughts to mankind, who turns dawn to darkness, and treads on the heights of the earth— the Lord God Almighty is his name."

Amos 4:13 NIV

It's simple.

- It's amazing to think that the omnipotent God who created the heavens and the earth speaks to us as humans.
- YOU can hear the voice of God.
- God wants to reveal His thoughts to you.
- Listen for the thoughts of God.
- God's thoughts are not your thoughts. (Isaiah 55:8)
- As my good friend Steve Sampson says, "One way to hear more from the Holy Spirit is to fast from our own thoughts."
- God is always speaking. Are you listening?
- God speaks to those who are close to Him and are listening.

God waits for you to communicate with Him. You have instant, direct access to God. God loves mankind so much, and in a very special sense His children, that He has made Himself available to you at all times.

— Wesley L. Duewel

Obadiah.

The King and His Kingdom.

And the kingdom will be the Lord's.

Obadiah 21b NIV

It's simple.

- Ultimately, God brings justice for His people.
- It may look like the bad guys are winning, but in the end God guarantees the victory.
- God will win because EVERYTHING belongs to Him.
- *"The earth is the Lord's, and everything in it. The world and all its people belong to him."* Psalms 24:1 NLT
- Prime Minister of the Netherlands and theologian, Abraham Kuyper said, "There is not a square inch in the whole domain of our human existence over which Christ, who is Sovereign over all, does not cry, Mine!"

God says we don't need to be anxious about anything: we just need to pray about everything.

— Stormie Omartian

Jonah.

God is slow to get angry.

So he complained to the Lord about it: "Didn't I say before I left home that you would do this, Lord? That is why I ran away to Tarshish! I knew that you are a merciful and compassionate God, slow to get angry and filled with unfailing love. You are eager to turn back from destroying people."

Jonah 4:2 NLT

It's simple.

- Jonah was a prophet.
- Jonah knew God.
- Jonah knew God is a God of grace.
- Jonah would preach.
- Nineveh would repent.
- God would relent.
- God always responds positively to true repentance.
- Jonah knew this.
- That's why he ran in the first place.
- Jonah knew God would ultimately forgive them.
- In our verse, Jonah shares the common refrain that describes our God.
- God is merciful.
- God is compassionate.
- God is patient.
- God is filled with unfailing love.
- God's heart is to bless, not curse.

God has no bad thoughts toward us.

— Graham Cooke

Micah.

What does God require of you.

"He has told you, O man, what is good; and what does the Lord require of you but to do justice, and to love kindness, and to walk humbly with your God?"

Micah 6:8 ESV

It's simple.

- God shoots straight with us in His Word.
- God tells us exactly what He requires of us.
- We don't have to guess at what God wants.
- What does God require of you?
- What will make God happy?
- Do justice.
- Justice simply means to treat people right.
- Tim Keller said, "We do justice when we give all human beings their due as creations of God."
- Don't just believe in justice, DO justice.
- Love kindness.
- Do justice with kindness.
- Kindness is one of the main characteristics of love. (see 1 Corinthians 13:4)
- Kindness literally means gentle behavior.
- Walk humbly with our God.
- We need God.
- God responds to our humility.
- When we pray with humility, God listens.
- *"For all those who exalt themselves will be humbled, and those who humble themselves will be exalted."* Luke18:14b

Spiritual disciplines are not about making you more precious to God. They're about making God more precious to you.

— Matt Smethurst

Nahum.

God is good.

"The Lord is good, a refuge in times of trouble. He cares for those who trust in him."

Nahum 1:7 NIV

It's simple.

- The prophet Nahum's name means comfort.
- The focus of his prophecy is God's judgment of Nineveh for its oppression, cruelty, idolatry, and wickedness.
- It's really Jonah Part 2.
- God is slow to get angry (see Nahum 1:3) but this time Nineveh won't repent.
- Nahum shows both the kindness and judgment of God.
- What do we learn about God?
- He is good.
- He is a refuge in times of trouble.
- He cares for those who trust in Him.

Do you believe that the God of Jesus loves you beyond worthiness and unworthiness, beyond fidelity and infidelity—that he loves you in the morning sun and in the evening rain—that he loves you when your intellect denies it, your emotions refuse it, your whole being rejects it. Do you believe that God loves without condition or reservation and loves you this moment as you are and not as you should be?

—Brennan Manning

Habakkuk.

God is your strength.

"Though the fig tree does not bud and there are no grapes on the vines, though the olive crop fails and the fields produce no food, though there are no sheep in the pen and no cattle in the stalls, yet I will rejoice in the Lord, I will be joyful in God my Savior. The Sovereign Lord is my strength; he makes my feet like the feet of a deer, he enables me to tread on the heights."
Habakkuk 3:17-19 NIV

It's simple.

- Habakkuk's world was full of violence and injustice.
- There were a lot of "why" questions.
- Even in the midst of it all, Habakkuk's message was God is still in control.
- Whether we sense it or not, God is working.
- We are to have faith even when God seems unresponsive.
- We are to worship and rejoice in God no matter what.
- He is our strength.
- He will be our rescue.
- He is God.

If you know that God loves you, you should never question a directive from Him. It will always be right and best. When He gives you a directive, you are not just to observe it, discuss it, or debate it. You are to obey it.

— Henry Blackaby

Zephaniah.

God takes great delight in you.

"The Lord your God is with you, the Mighty Warrior who saves. He will take great delight in you; in his love he will no longer rebuke you, but will rejoice over you with singing."
Zephaniah 3:17 NIV

It's simple.

- Zephaniah (and all of God's Word) tells us the "Day of the Lord" is coming and with it is great judgement.
- But for those who listen to God, repent, and follow there is no fear of the "Day of the Lord."
- In fact, God takes care of you no matter the situation.
- He is with you.
- He will save you.
- He takes great delight in you.
- There is no more rebuke, only rejoicing.
- That's really good news.

God is madly in love with you.

— Good Grace, United

Haggai.

He is a God of peace.

"Be strong, all you people of the land," declares the Lord, "and work. For I am with you," declares the Lord Almighty.
Haggai 2:4 NIV

It's simple.

- The Jews are returning from exile and Haggai is compelling them to rebuild the destroyed temple.
- Make God and His Word your priority.
- When you put God first He WILL bless you.
- Be strong and work for the Lord.
- He is with you.
- He will give you peace.

The less time you spend with the truth, the easier it is to believe lies.

— Lecrae

Zechariah.

Return to Me.

Therefore tell the people: This is what the Lord Almighty says: "Return to me," declares the Lord Almighty, "and I will return to you," says the Lord Almighty.
Zechariah 1:3 NIV

It's simple.

- Like Haggai, Zechariah is calling God's people to rebuild the temple.
- It's not about the past.
- No matter how far you have strayed from God you can always return to Him.
- And when you return to Him, He will return to you.

For me to prepare my heart means that I come to Him in adoration first. I don't come with a need for a message. I come in adoration out of desire to be with Him. And I would rather have nothing to say and be current in my fellowship with Him than to have lots to say and be trying to find Him. That's the main thing for me—I make sure that I am current...that my relationship is fresh. It's about feeling His pleasure, which is the awareness of His heart.

— Bill Johnson

Malachi.

The Lord honors those who fear Him.

"On the day when I act," says the Lord Almighty, "they will be my treasured possession. I will spare them, just as a father has compassion and spares his son who serves him."
Malachi 3:17 NIV

It's simple.

- Malachi prophesies a century after Haggai and Zechariah.
- In that time, God's people had become lax in their worship and relationship with God.
- When God becomes distant, so does His blessings and favor.
- For the remnant that feared the Lord, He listened and heard their cry.
- Keep that close relationship with God and you will be His treasured possession.
- You will know His rescue and compassion.

NEW TESTAMENT

I believe the Bible is the best gift God has ever given to man. All the good from The Savior of the world is communicated to us through this Book.

— Abraham Lincoln

Matthew.

Savior.

"She will give birth to a son, and you are to give him the name Jesus, because he will save his people from their sins."

Matthew 1:21 NIV

It's simple.

- Jesus arrives on the pages of the New Covenant and His purpose is made clear right away.
- Jesus came to be our Savior.
- That's why God came near.
- We need to be saved from our sins.
- Matthew knew he needed forgiveness.
- He was a tax collector.
- He was an outcast.
- He wouldn't have been allowed close to the temple.
- No friends and no access to God.
- He was on the outside looking in.
- Yet Jesus went out of His way to save Matthew.
- Matthew's message became one of forgiveness.
- God is our Savior who forgives.
- That is good news!

Loving people the way Jesus did is great theology.

— Bob Goff

Mark.

Serve.

"For even the Son of Man did not come to be served, but to serve, and to give his life as a ransom for many."
Mark 10:45 NIV

It's simple.

- Even in His omnipotence, God chose to serve.
- When God entered our world, in Jesus, He didn't come as a master but as a servant.
- God didn't show up to judge, He showed up to save.
- God gave all of Himself for you and me.
- When Jesus calls us to follow Him, He's asking us to serve others as He did.

Jesus didn't go around condemning people. The Bible says it's the goodness of God that leads people to repentance.

— Joel Osteen

Luke.

Prodigal God.

"For the Son of Man came to seek and to save the lost."

Luke 19:10 NIV

It's simple.

- Jesus would go out of His way to be with people who needed him.
- That's why Jesus said he "must" meet with Zacchaeus in Luke 19.
- Zacchaeus didn't deserve it.
- Zacchaeus couldn't buy or earn Jesus' attention.
- Zacchaeus was living with the shame of being hated by everyone and feeling unforgivable.
- God's heart is for those who need Him.
- Jesus goes and shares a meal with Zacchaeus.
- Sharing a meal with someone in Jesus' time was a sign of relationship.
- That meal changed Zacchaeus forever.
- Zacchaeus experienced God's love, joy, peace, generosity, help, hospitality, and most of all His grace.
- It was God's unconditional love that moved Zacchaeus to repentance and salvation.
- It's simple, this is why God came to earth, "to seek and save the lost."

God proved His love on the Cross. When Christ hung, and bled, and died, it was God saying to the world, "I love you."

— Billy Graham

John.

Love.

"For God so loved the world that He gave His only begotten Son, that whoever believes in Him should not perish but have everlasting life. For God did not send His Son into the world to condemn the world, but that the world through Him might be saved."

John 3:16-17 NKJV

It's simple.

- John writes his Gospel to tell us who Jesus is and why He came.
- Could the heart of God be more clear?
- God LOVES the world.
- God loves EVERYONE.
- Jesus (God in the flesh) didn't come into the world to condemn the world.
- Jesus came to save the world.
- Jesus came to be your Savior.
- God wants to save you!
- Believing leads to eternal life.
- Following and obedience leads to abundant life.

You are a habitation of God. There is no separation. He will never leave you. He will never forsake you. He is always with you.

— Graham Cooke

Acts.

The goodness of God.

"...but he never left them without evidence of himself and his goodness. For instance, he sends you rain and good crops and gives you food and joyful hearts."
Acts 14:17 NLT

It's simple.

- In the Book of Acts God pours out His Spirit on all flesh.
- There is so much about the church, our spiritual life, and the power of the Holy Spirit in Acts.
- In this verse, Paul is sharing the goodness of God.
- God is continually revealing Himself to the world.
- God loves everyone and is good to all, even before they know Him.
- God is a good provider.
- He provides for our physical and emotional needs.

We should be astonished at the goodness of God, stunned that He should bother to call us by name, our mouths wide open at His love, bewildered that at this very moment we are standing on holy ground.

— Brennan Manning

Romans.

God works everything together for our good.

We know that God works all things together for good for the ones who love God, for those who are called according to his purpose.
Romans 8:28 CEB

It's simple.

- God has assigned an outcome to every circumstance in your life, and it is GOOD.
- God works ALL THINGS together for good, not just some.
- God is at work in every situation and stage of your life and it is good.
- God is at work spiritually, mentally, and physically.
- There is no more condemnation. (see Romans 8:1)
- God is making you righteous. (see Romans 5:19)
- You are dead to sin. (see Romans 6:7)
- God is renewing your mind. (see Romans 12:2)
- If God is for us, who can be against us. (see Romans 8:31)
- We are victorious. (see Romans 8:37)
- There is NOTHING that can separate you from the love of God. (see Romans 8:38-39)

Jesus is not your accuser. He's not your prosecutor. He's not your judge. He's your friend and your rescuer. Like Zacchaeus, just spend time with Jesus. Don't hide from him in shame or reject him in self-righteousness. Don't allow the opinions of other people to shape your concept of him. Get to know him for yourself, and let the goodness of God change you from the inside out.

— Judah Smith

1 Corinthians.

Remember.

...the Lord Jesus on the night when he was betrayed took bread, and when he had given thanks, he broke it, and said, "This is my body, which is for you. Do this in remembrance of me." In the same way also he took the cup, after supper, saying, "This cup is the new covenant in my blood. Do this, as often as you drink it, in remembrance of me."

1 Corinthians 11:23b-25 NIV

It's simple.

- When Jesus inaugurates Communion, He tells us we are partaking to remember Him.
- You're not to remember your past.
- You're not to remember your brokenness.
- You're not to remember your sin.
- You're to simply remember Jesus.
- What He did.
- His sacrifice.
- His love.
- His victory.
- He went to the cross for YOU.
- How do you receive His forgiveness?
- How do you receive His love?
- How do you partake in His victory?
- You don't have to do anything but remember Him.
- What He has done.
- It is finished.

Many stop short of an encounter because they're satisfied with good theology. Truth is supposed to lead to a person.

— Bill Johnson

2 Corinthians.

Grace.

But he said to me, "My grace is sufficient for you, for my power is made perfect in weakness." Therefore I will boast all the more gladly about my weaknesses, so that Christ's power may rest on me.

2 Corinthians 12:9 NIV

It's simple.

- 2 Corinthians is the most personal of all of Paul's letters.
- He shares all that he's been through. (see 2 Cor. 11:24-29)
- Shipwrecks. Beatings. Imprisonments. Dangers. Weakness. Persecution. Hardships were aplenty.
- Paul mentions a "thorn in the flesh" that he prayed would be taken away.
- God's answer was that the "thorn" would continue but God's grace would be sufficient.
- We don't have to ask God to make His grace sufficient. It already is.
- When we are weak, God is strong.
- No wonder Paul boasted in his weakness.
- Paul knew his weakness would bring the power of God to his life.
- Sometimes we pray for relief, but God wants to increase our strength.
- God wants His power and grace on display in our lives.
- *"But we have this treasure in jars of clay, to show that the surpassing power belongs to God and not to us."*
2 Corinthians 4:7

We find in Jesus a God that supports us from underneath in grace rather than a God dangling us from above in wrath.

— AJ Sherrill

Galatians.

Sowing and Reaping.

Do not be deceived: God cannot be mocked. A man reaps what he sows. Whoever sows to please their flesh, from the flesh will reap destruction; whoever sows to please the Spirit, from the Spirit will reap eternal life. Let us not become weary in doing good, for at the proper time we will reap a harvest if we do not give up.

Galatians 6:7-9 NIV

It's simple.

- God gives us warnings, but He also gives us blessings.
- He makes things crystal clear.
- There are no surprises when it comes to the law of sowing and reaping.
- There are consequences to our actions.
- You can live according to the flesh or according to the Spirit.
- Please the flesh and reap destruction.
- Please the Holy Spirit and reap eternal life.
- Do good.
- Don't give up.
- A good harvest is coming.
- God wants you to know and understand the law of sowing and reaping.
- God, the Holy Spirit, is there for you.
- Follow Him and reap the blessings.

Some Christians base their identity on being a sinner. I think they have it wrong – or only half right. You are not simply a sinner; you are a deeply loved sinner. And there is all the difference in the world between the two.

— David Benner

Ephesians.

Masterpiece.

For we are God's masterpiece. He has created us anew in Christ Jesus, so we can do the good things he planned for us long ago.

Ephesians 2:10 NLT

It's simple.

- You are God's masterpiece.
- You are His work of art.
- *"And yet, O Lord, you are our Father. We are the clay, and you are the potter. We all are formed by your hand."*
  Isaiah 64:8 NLT
- God not only created you with exactly what you need, but He's also at work shaping you into exactly what you were created to be.
- He won't give up on you.
- God created you with purpose.
- You were created for a purpose.
- Mark Batterson reminds us, "There never has been and never will be anyone like you. But that isn't a testament to you. It's a testament to the God who created you."
- If Almighty God created you that special, He must have something extremely important for you to do.
- Discover the exclusive reason for which you were created.
- Then be faithful and obedient to God and His purpose for your life.

All God's giants have been weak men and women who have gotten hold of God's faithfulness.

— Hudson Taylor

Philippians.

Joy.

Rejoice in the Lord always. I will say it again: Rejoice!
                                        Philippians 4:4 NIV

It's simple.
- Everyone wants to be happy. Right? So rejoice!
- Joy is the theme of Paul's life and the letter to his friends, the Philippians.
- Even though Paul was in prison, even though he didn't know if he would be freed or martyred, even in all of this, he told us to "rejoice in the Lord."
- Our joy is not based on our circumstances.
- Circumstances change all the time.
- Our joy is grounded in something much deeper.
- Our joy is based in our relationship with God.
- Paul tells us, *"Do not be anxious about anything, but in every situation, by prayer and petition, with thanksgiving, present your requests to God."* (Philippians 4:6)
- If we do, *"the peace of God, which transcends all understanding, will guard your hearts and your minds in Christ Jesus."* (Philippians 4:7)
- Paul teaches us to THINK ourselves joyful.
- *"Finally, brothers and sisters, whatever is true, whatever is noble, whatever is right, whatever is pure, whatever is lovely, whatever is admirable—if anything is excellent or praiseworthy—think about such things."* (Philippians 4:8)
- Paul's joy was based in knowing Christ alone. (Phil. 3:10)
- This is the secret of a joyful Christian life.
- Our joy is based on sharing our life with Him, communicating with Him, depending on Him, and thinking His thoughts.
- God is a God of delight and enjoyment.

God loves each of us as if there were only one of us.

— Augustine

Colossians.

Complete.

So you also are complete through your union with Christ, who is the head over every ruler and authority.
                                    Colossians 2:10 NLT

It's simple.

- Jesus is God.
- He is supreme.
- *"His power extends over EVERYTHING."*
  Colossians 2:10 MSG
- There is NOTHING more powerful than Jesus.
- All and everything are in submission to Him.
- You are IN Him.
- In Him you are COMPLETE.
- "Complete" in Paul's original language meant "full, perfect, reaching maximum spiritual capacity."
- Everything you need is found in Jesus.
- There's no reason to look anywhere else.
- Anything else is just a cheap counterfeit to the real thing.
- Is Jesus dominant in your life?
- He can transform everything in your life.
- Look to Jesus today.
- Walk in relationship.
- Allow His power to be at work in your life.
- He is all you need!

Attack anything that makes you feel unworthy, inadequate, hopeless, powerless and useless. That is the evidence of the enemy. All those things need to be attacked with joy, with peace, with love and grace, with mercy, with kindness and the goodness of God.

— Graham Cooke

1 Thessalonians.

Salvation.

For God did not appoint us to suffer wrath but to receive salvation through our Lord Jesus Christ.

1 Thessalonians 5:9 NIV

It's simple.

- God is a God of help, rescue, and salvation.
- God appointed you to be saved.
- Suffering His wrath isn't for you.
- Jesus made the way to present you blameless through His work on the cross.
- Jesus is at work in you.
- *"May he strengthen your hearts so that you will be blameless and holy in the presence of our God and Father when our Lord Jesus comes with all his holy ones."*
 1 Thessalonians 3:13

Great is Thy faithfulness
Morning by morning new mercies I see
And all I have needed Thy hand hath provided
Great is Thy faithfulness
Lord unto me

— Thomas Chisholm

2 Thessalonians.

Protection.

But the Lord is faithful, and he will strengthen you and protect you from the evil one.

2 Thessalonians 3:3 NIV

It's simple.

- In this short book of the Bible, there is a lot of talk of the evil and harshness of the "end times."
- No matter the situation, God is faithful.
- No matter what is happening to you or around you, God will give you strength.
- No matter what the evil one intends to do, God will protect you.
- Whether it's your everyday life or the "end of the world," God's got you covered.
- Live with that expectation.

The forbearance and long-suffering of God towards sinners is truly astonishing.

— Benjamin Beddome

1 Timothy.

Destined to be saved.

Here is a trustworthy saying that deserves full acceptance: Christ Jesus came into the world to save sinners—of whom I am the worst.

1 Timothy 1:15 NIV

It's simple.

- The purpose of God coming to earth was to save sinners.
- This is a reframe that begins in the Gospels and continues throughout the New Testament.
- Paul, in essence, is saying, "You can take it to the bank…"
- Jesus came to save you, me, Paul, all of us, because we are all sinners.
- God's love and salvation are aimed at you.
- All it is takes on your part is repentance.
- When confronted with his sin, Paul didn't make excuses or give explanations.
- He recognized the depth of his sinfulness, repented, and God turned his life completely around.
- You were destined to be saved.
- Jesus came for YOU!
- Your response? Repent and turn from your sin.

God's faithfulness means that God will always do what He said and fulfill what He has promised.

— Wayne Grudem

2 Timothy.

Fear doesn't come from God.

For God has not given us a spirit of fear, but of power and of love and of a sound mind.

2 Timothy 1:7 NKJV

It's simple.

- God's key command throughout the Bible is, "Do not be afraid."
- Fear doesn't come from God.
- The enemy uses fear to steal, kill, and destroy.
- We are to trust in the God who overcomes the enemy and gives us power, love, and self-discipline.
- If we are in right relationship with God there is nothing to fear.
- God gives us His mighty power to overcome fear.
- The perfect love of God casts out all fear. (see 1 John 4:18)
- The Holy Spirit produces self-discipline in us to conquer the fear that the enemy uses to destroy us.
- Paul writes this verse while facing martyrdom, proving even in the most difficult times in life, we do not need to be fearful or timid.

The glory of God's faithfulness is that no sin of ours has ever made Him unfaithful.

— Charles Spurgeon

Titus.

Eternal Life. New life.

...in the hope of eternal life, which God, who does not lie, promised before the beginning of time.
Titus 1:2 NIV

It's simple.

- God has promised eternal life.
- It's been a part of His plan for you and me from the very beginning.
- God does not lie.
- His promises are Yes and Amen. (see 2 Corinthians 1:20)
- So how does God's plan work?
- *"But when the kindness and love of God our Savior appeared, he saved us, not because of righteous things we had done, but because of his mercy. He saved us through the washing of rebirth and renewal by the Holy Spirit, whom he poured out on us generously through Jesus Christ our Savior, so that, having been justified by his grace, we might become heirs having the hope of eternal life."*
Titus 3:4-7 NIV
- And Titus tells us WHY God saves us.
- To redeem us.
- To purify us.
- To make us His own.
- So that we can do what is good.
- *"Who gave himself for us to redeem us from all wickedness and to purify for himself a people that are his very own, eager to do what is good."* Titus 2:14 NIV

A saint is not someone who is good but who experiences the goodness of God.

— Brennan Manning

Philemon.

Reconciliation.

Perhaps the reason he was separated from you for a little while was that you might have him back forever— no longer as a slave, but better than a slave, as a dear brother. He is very dear to me but even dearer to you, both as a fellow man and as a brother in the Lord.
Philemon 1:15-16 NIV

It's simple.

- Forgiveness and reconciliation is foundational to the Christian life.
- The book of Philemon is all about forgiveness and reconciliation.
- Specifically, reconciling a runaway slave to his owner.
- Not reconciling to the old relationship of slave and master but to a new relationship of brother and friend because of Christ.
- This is mind-blowing!
- Jesus changes everything.
- His Kingdom isn't like the kingdoms of this world.
- *"There is neither Jew nor Gentile, neither slave nor free, nor is there male and female, for you are all one in Christ Jesus."* Galatians 3:28 NIV
- In Christ, we have a new identity.
- The old is gone and the new has come.
- We belong to God.
- And that changes everything!

Jesus loved people others rejected - even people who rejected him. This is how God loves.

— Gregory A. Boyd

Hebrews.

Never alone.

For God has said, "I will never fail you. I will never abandon you."

Hebrews 13:5b NLT

It's simple.

- God has a covenant of everlasting presence with you.
- God is with you.
- God's got you.
- God won't fail you.
- God will never abandon you.
- Never doubt it.
- Hebrews teaches us the supremacy of Jesus.
- There is nothing better than Jesus.
- He is both our great high priest and the perfect sacrifice.
- He takes care of everything!
- The good news is He will never leave us or forsake us.
- Put your faith in Christ.

God's greatest attribute is not his power, though it is omniscience; not his glory, though it is burning majesty: it is his love.

— Al Bryant

James.

God's heart is for the humble.

God opposes the proud but shows favor to the humble.
                                        James 4:6b NIV

It's simple.

- There is a theme throughout the Bible.
- It shows up again in James.
- God opposes the proud.
- God gives grace to the humble.
- If you're proud, you're an enemy of God.
- If you're humble, you're a friend of God.
- James teaches in his letter to walk humbly with God and people.
- Our hearts, tongue, and actions should always demonstrate true humility.
- God's heart is always for the humble.

By the time kids are five I want them to know three things - God made me. God loves me. Jesus wants to be my friend forever.

— Carey Nieuwhof

1 Peter.

God cares about what you care about.

Cast all your anxiety on him because he cares for you.
                                                    1 Peter 5:7 NIV

It's simple.

- This is the very first verse I memorized as a young boy.
- Little did I know it would become a lifeline when I would suffer from anxiety later in life.
- God cares for us.
- He watches out for those He loves.
- The readers of Peter's letter were experiencing the harshest persecution.
- Many were losing everything.
- Some were losing their lives.
- There was much to worry about.
- They had reason to be anxious.
- They also had a great deal to rejoice in.
- God loved them.
- They belonged to God.
- He was watching out for them.
- And no matter what happened, God ultimately was going to take good care of them.
- *"But you are a chosen people, a royal priesthood, a holy nation, God's special possession, that you may declare the praises of him who called you out of darkness into his wonderful light."* 1 Peter 2:9 NIV

There's no place too dark for God's light to penetrate and no heart too difficult to be set aflame by His love.

— Sammy Tippit

2 Peter.

God has given us everything we need.

His divine power has given us everything we need for a godly life through our knowledge of him who called us by his own glory and goodness. Through these he has given us his very great and precious promises, so that through them you may participate in the divine nature, having escaped the corruption in the world caused by evil desires.
2 Peter 1:3-4 NIV

It's simple.

- God has given us everything we need for a godly life.
- The power of this godly life doesn't come from within us but from God.
- It comes from knowing the glory and goodness of God and His Spirit at work inside of us.
- God had made precious, divine promises.
- Promises He will keep because we belong to Him.
- We don't belong to this corrupt world or evil desires.
- We belong to God.

God is a God of the present. God is always in the moment, be that moment hard or easy, joyful and painful.

— Henri Nouwen

1 John.

If/Then.

If we confess our sins, he is faithful and just and will forgive us our sins and purify us from all unrighteousness.

1 John 1:9 NIV

It's simple.

- There are a lot of IF/THEN statements in the Bible.
- We need to pay attention to each of them because God always keeps His word.
- This verse holds a tremendous promise.
- IF we confess, THEN God will forgive.
- We could never pay the price to purify our sin.
- We are simply guilty with no way out.
- Yet God is faithful to forgive 100% of our sin.
- All we have to do is confess our sins to Him and He does all the rest.
- God wants to see us set free, forgiven, and in relationship with Him.
- Confess your sins and you will be forgiven!
- This is God's covenant promise!

Long ago I came to the total assurance that God loves me, God knows where I am every second of every day, and God is bigger than any problem life's circumstances can throw at me.

— Charles Stanley

2 John.

The simple commandment of love.

And this is love: that we walk in obedience to his commands. As you have heard from the beginning, his command is that you walk in love.
2 John 1:6 NIV

It's simple.

- The Bible is full of laws and commands.
- Because of this, we think there are a lot of "rules" to following God and therefore God is hard to please.
- But Jesus reduces all of the commands of Scripture to one thing… love.
- The two greatest commands are to love God and love others. (see Mark 12:30-31)
- Paul says in Romans 13:10b, *"Therefore love is the fulfillment of the law."*
- So it's simple, to walk in obedience to God's commands means to walk in love.

All of us can look back and see things that should have defeated us. You're still standing. That's the goodness of God.

— Joel Osteen

3 John.

God wants you to prosper.

Dear friend, I pray that you may enjoy good health and that all may go well with you, even as your soul is getting along well.

3 John 1:2 NIV

It's simple.

- God wants you to prosper.
- He wants you to prosper in every area of your life.
- Remember what Jesus said, *"The thief comes only to steal and kill and destroy. I came that they may have life and have it abundantly."* John 10:10 ESV
- God is a God of abundance.
- God is a good Father who listens to our prayers and wants to bless His children.
- Walk in the truth of God's Word and embrace your abundant life in Him.
- *"I have no greater joy than to hear that my children are walking in the truth."* 3 John 1:4 NIV

God knows when to send exactly what you need.

— Daryl Merrill

Jude.

God's got you.

To him who is able to keep you from stumbling and to present you before his glorious presence without fault and with great joy— to the only God our Savior be glory, majesty, power and authority, through Jesus Christ our Lord, before all ages, now and forevermore! Amen.

Jude 1:24-25 NIV

It's simple.

- This is one of the most beautiful doxologies in the Bible.
- A doxology is praise, honor, and glory given to God.
- In this passage God is praised for His everlasting glory, majesty, power, and authority.
- What does this mean for you and me?
- Our powerful God is able to keep us, protect us, and sanctify us so we are forgiven and ready to spend a joyful eternity with Him.
- What a great God!
- Amen.

Jesus loves me this I know, for the Bible tells me so.

— Anna Bartlett Warner

Revelation.

In the end, it's all about relationship.

Here I am! I stand at the door and knock. If anyone hears my voice and opens the door, I will come in and eat with that person, and they with me.
Revelation 3:20 NIV

It's simple.

- This last book of the Bible gives us a glimpse of things to come.
- In the end, God ultimately wins and sets everything right.
- He will come again, wipe away every tear, and set up a perfect eternity with Him.
- In this final book we are reminded of the simple truth we see throughout His Word.
- All God wants is a relationship with you.
- He's knocking.
- He's calling.
- He's waiting.
- Patiently.
- If you open the door of your heart, He will come in.
- You can be in relationship with Jesus today and forever.
- Invite Jesus in today.

I beg of you, my dear brother [and sisters], to live among these books [Scriptures], to meditate upon them, to know nothing else, to seek nothing else.

— St. Jerome

A FINAL THOUGHT

You were made for a relationship with God. That relationship will not only impact your everyday life it will determine your ultimate destiny. God is good and He loves you! It's time to connect with and get to know the God of the Bible.

I hope God has come alive to you through the verses I have shared. There is SO MUCH MORE for you to discover. Dive into God's Word to discover more.

A SALVATION PRAYER

It's simple. God loves you. He wants a relationship with you. He wants to adopt you as His beloved son or daughter. And He's done everything necessary to make that happen. Now it's up to you to believe and receive. Say this prayer today.

Dear Lord Jesus, I know that I am a sinner and need Your forgiveness. I believe that you love me. I believe that You died for my sins. I want to turn from my sins. I now invite You to come into my heart and life. I want to trust and follow You as Lord and Savior. In Jesus' name. Amen.

ABOUT THE AUTHOR

Daryl is a husband, father, pastor and teacher.

He loves seeing people grow deeper in their relationship with God, embrace their true identity, and reach their full potential.

Daryl is Lead Pastor of Christian Life Church and Vice President of Christian Life College.

He did his doctoral work at Oxford University and post doctoral studies at Yale Divinity School and Princeton Seminary.

Through the church, college, and various mission organizations he has had the opportunity to travel the world teaching the Bible.

You can find out and read more at www.darylmerrill.com.

ALSO AVAILABLE ON AMAZON

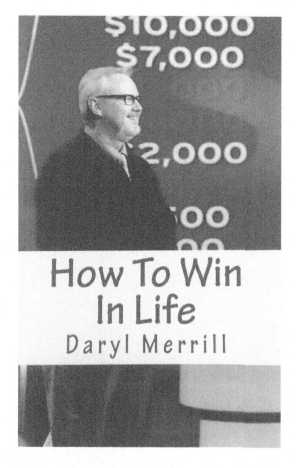

"Once upon a time, I was a contestant on the TV game show 'Who Wants To Be A Millionaire?' It was an extraordinary experience, but the things I enjoyed the most were the encouragement and cheers I felt from family and friends. While I didn't win a million dollars, I had a blast and learned a lot about winning along the way."

In this book, Daryl will share with you 12 LIFE LESSONS about winning in life he learned from his "Millionaire" experience.

Made in the USA
Monee, IL
20 April 2021